Maps

Written by Karen Wallace
Illustrated by Giorgio Bacchin

Collins

This map comes from 8000 years back!
It is painted on rock.

Some maps from 600 years back were painted on cloth. They had monsters and mermaids on.

Explorers and travellers 500 years back took fleets of ships on long trips.

The travellers and explorers went on quests to lands they had not yet seen.

The explorers' trips led to clearer maps. There were no mermaids or monsters, but hills, rivers and coasts.

Astronomers had maps of the stars and planets.

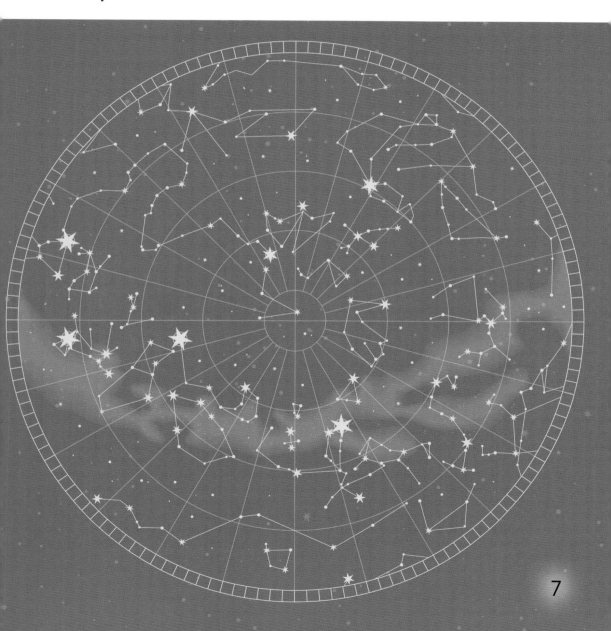

There are lots of sorts of maps.
This is a map of the continents.

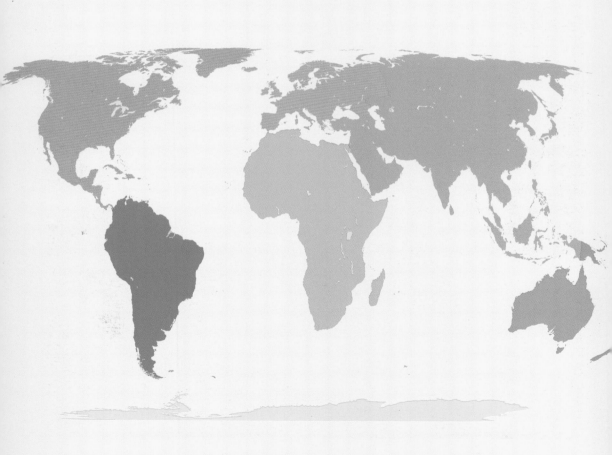

Street maps help us to get from a starting point to an end point.

Maps have clear marks so we can spot what is there.

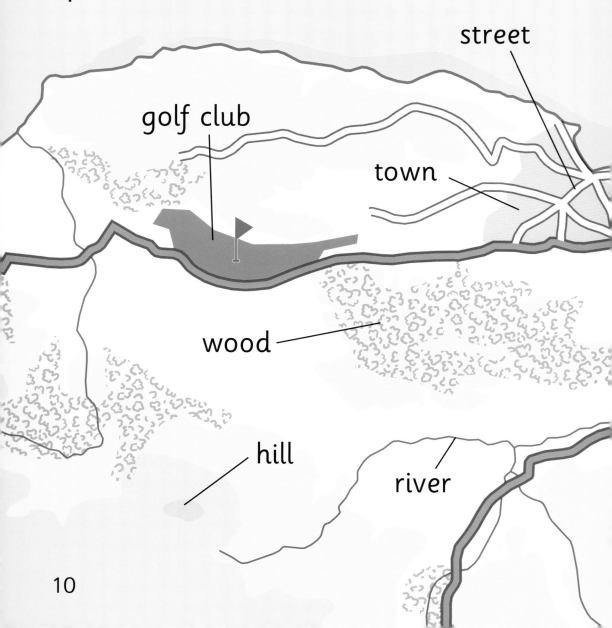

street

golf club

town

wood

hill

river

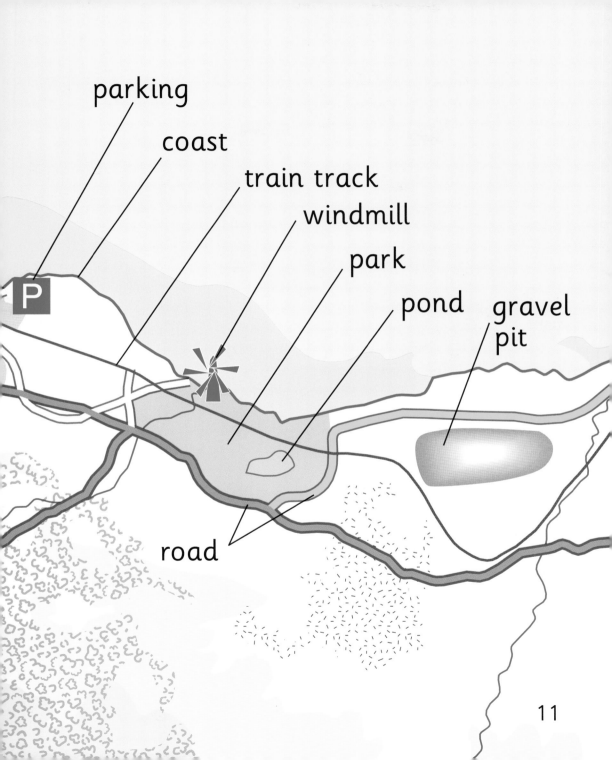

parking

coast

train track

windmill

park

pond

gravel pit

road

P

11

Smart maps help to keep us on track, so we do not get lost.

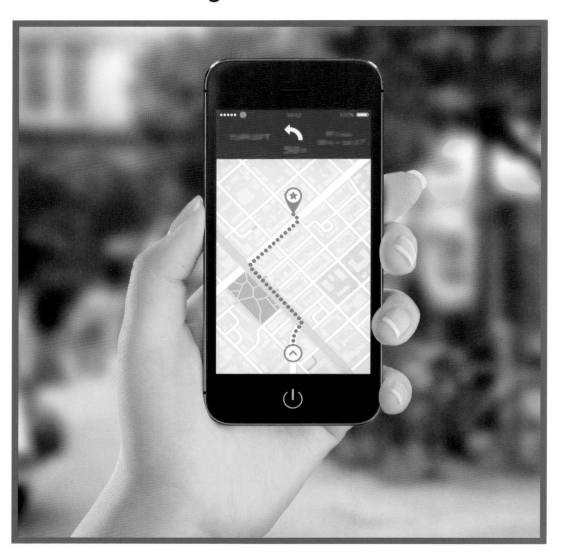

Maps help us to understand the planet.
Now we can be explorers too!

Maps

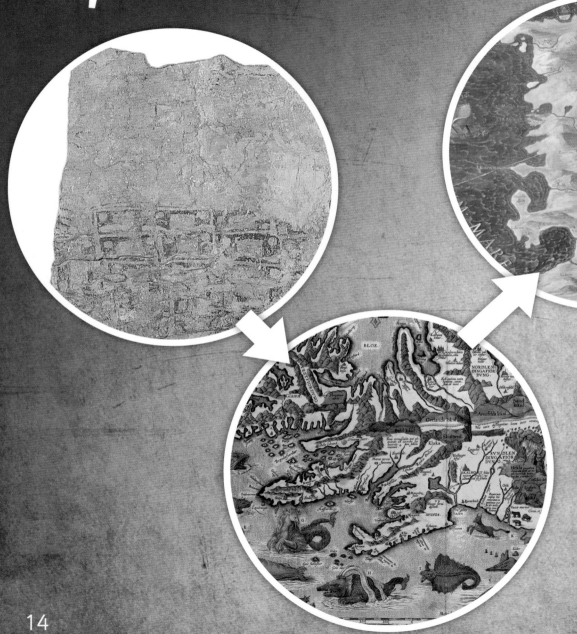

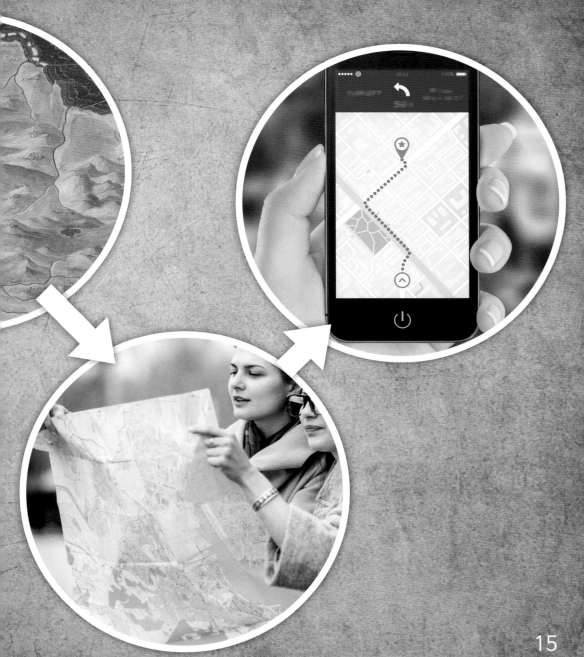

⁙ Review: After reading ⁙

Use your assessment from hearing the children read to choose any GPCs, words or tricky words that need additional practice.

Read 1: Decoding

- Model sounding out the following word, saying each of the sounds quickly and clearly. Then blend the sounds together. Ask the children to do the same.

  s/t/r/ee/t   street

- Ask the children:
  - Point to the beginning three letters in the word **street**. Can you think of any other words that begin with these three letters "s" "t" "r"? (e.g. *stream, stripe*)
  - Now think of some more words that include the bold letters in the words below.

    pai**nt**   **cl**ear   **st**art

Read 2: Prosody

- Choose two double page spreads and model reading with expression to the children.
- Ask the children to have a go at reading the same pages with expression.

Read 3: Comprehension

- Turn to pages 14 and 15 and ask the children to explain to you how maps have changed over time.
- For every question ask the children how they know the answer. Ask:
  - What were the first maps like? (*they were simple and drawn on rock*)
  - What did astronomers have maps of? (*stars and planets*)
  - What is the most interesting or surprising thing you found out from this book?